CRITICAL RACE THEORY

A Doctrine of Devils That Is Captivating the Minds of Americans

By
David L. Brown, Ph.D.

ISBN 978-1-7356723-5-9

All Scripture quotes are from the King James Bible.

Address All Inquiries To:
THE OLD PATHS PUBLICATIONS, Inc.
142 Gold Flume Way
Cleveland, Georgia, U.S.A. 30528

Web: www.theoldpathspublications.com
E-mail: TOP@theoldpathspublications.com

The front cover photo is by Vahine Nefertare at www.pinterest.com/pin/397724210812355923/visual-search/ Dr. Brown is thankful to be able to use it.

TABLE OF CONTENTS

There is a passage of Scripture that I want to share with you before I address what is called the Critical Race Theory.

1 Timothy 4:1-2:

> *"Now the Spirit speaketh expressly, that in the latter times some shall depart from the faith, <u>giving heed to seducing spirits, and doctrines of devils</u>; 2 Speaking lies in hypocrisy; having their conscience seared with a hot iron;"*

INTRODUCTION

The agitation of the Black Lives Matter movement has dominated the public discourse in the United States since the death of an African American man who died during his arrest in Minneapolis. This was a tragic event. The death of Mr. Floyd was troubling indeed. However, I am also concerned over the legitimacy of the phrase "black lives matter," since all lives irrespective of race matter! Mr. Floyd's death was the spark that lit the fires of violent protests, police shootings and terrorism in many cities across the USA by groups like Black Lives Matter, Antifa and other groups and individuals. In fact, violence is being encouraged. One Black Lives Matter leader said they would burn the system down if they don't get what they want. When Philadelphia Police shot and killed Walter Wallace who refused to drop his knife and came at them October 26, 2020 people marched through the streets shouting, "Every city every town, burn the precincts to the ground." Following was looting and violence where 30 policemen were injured.

What is at the root of all of this? I believe the foundation of all of this is a philosophy called **Critical Race Theory.**

Back in the early 70's there was a movement among liberal scholars in American law that was very obscure. It was known as The Critical Race Theory (CRT). This theory was based on the Critical Theory which was a Marxist-inspired movement in social and political philosophy first defined by Max Horkheimer of the Frankfurt School of Sociology in his 1937 essay, *Traditional and Critical Theory.* He said that the aim of all critical theory is to "create a world which satisfies the needs and powers of human beings" (see Critical Theory 1972, p. 246).

Horkheimer drew from Karl Marx and Sigmund Freud and developed a philosophy to change society as a whole, overcoming current social structures through which people were dominated and oppressed. You could call it an emancipatory form of Marxism which overturns capitalism by revolution and replaces it with communism. The Critical Theory teaches that science, like other forms of knowledge, has been used as an instrument of oppression and they caution against a blind faith in scientific progress, arguing that scientific knowledge must not be pursued as an end in itself without reference to the goal of human emancipation. The _Critical Theory_ birthed the _Critical Race Theory_ which is like a fast spreading virus infecting nearly every area of society; education at every level, government, religion, the media, the work place and more.

THE DEFINITION OF
CRITICAL RACE THEORY
(CRT)

"**CRT** is the view that the law and legal institutions are inherently racist and that race itself, instead of being biologically grounded and natural, is a socially constructed concept that is used by white people to further their economic and political interests at the expense of people of colour."

(https://www.britannica.com/topic/critical-race-theory)

In CRT "Each individual is seen either as oppressed or as an oppressor, depending on their race, class, gender, sexuality, and a number of other categories. Oppressed groups are subjugated, not by physical force or even overt discrimination, but through the exercise of hegemonic power—the ability of dominant groups to impose their norms, values, and expectations on society as a whole, relegating other groups to subordinate positions."
(www.thegospelcoalition.org/article/incompatibility-critical-theory-christianity)

THE TEACHINGS OF CRT

THE FIRST TEACHING

- <u>**Racism is present in every aspect of life,**</u> **every relationship, and every interaction; therefore its** <u>**advocates look for it everywhere**</u>**!**

What you need to understand is that advocates of CRT use semantic word games to support their fraudulent theory. One way they do this is by <u>redefining **_racism_**</u> to fit their agenda. **What they mean by "racism" is not what most people think racism means**. <u>It is **not** prejudice based upon race or believing some races to be superior or inferior to others</u> that they mean by "racism." It is, instead, **the "system" of everything that happens in the social world and beyond, that results in any disparity that works in the favor of "racially privileged" groups (on average) or any "racially oppressed" person claiming they experience racial oppression**.

What advocates of CRT are saying is that <u>**the basic human problem is racism**</u>! They look for it everywhere and YOU must look for it also **or** <u>you are a racist</u>. You have to find and focus upon the "hidden" racism in your workplace, your school, your society, your

9

neighborhood, your books, your food, your music, your hobbies, your faith, your church, your community, your friends, your relationships, and yourself (and everything else too) all the time.

Their answer to the problem is that "woke" [woke=being alert to injustice in society, especially racism] whites join people of color in tearing down the existing system and replacing it with a new structure run by people of color.

Biblically, there are several MAJOR problems with their teaching. **First** of all, I remind you that this is a *theory*. Let me define **theory** for you. A **theory** is "a supposition or a system of ideas intended to explain something." The Merriam-Webster Dictionary online says a **theory** is "a plausible or scientifically acceptable general principle or body of principles offered to explain phenomena. A **theory** is an unproved assumption. Synonyms for theory are **speculation** and **conjecture**."

Paul warned in **1 Timothy 6:20,**

"O Timothy, keep that which is committed to thy trust, avoiding profane and vain babblings, and oppositions of science falsely so called." .

POINT ONE

CRT is a theory. It is **conjecture**. It is **speculation**. It is NOT science. It is not proved. It is built on a faulty supposition. Followers of this theory are trying to pass this off as truth. A lot of time and money is being spent by government, schools and workplaces to indoctrinate and brainwash people. Their objective is to convince people that their THEORY is TRUTH **when it is not**.

POINT TWO

This brings me to my **next point**. The advocates of this theory of victimization make broad sweeping declarations claiming **"everyone"** is a racist and racism is "everywhere." It is always dangerous to say "everyone" does this or that, or "no one" believes this or that. The Bible warns that we are to judge ourselves before we judge others (**Matthew 7:1-5**). Since they claim everyone is a "racist" and "racism" is everywhere; that would mean that they are racists and involved in racist activities. In a very real sense, they are. It is racism in reverse. Therefore they ARE GUILTY and inexcusable.

The Bible says in **Romans 2:1**,

"Therefore thou art inexcusable, O man, whosoever thou art that judgest: for wherein thou judgest another, thou condemnest thyself; for thou that judgest doest the same things."

POINT THREE

My **third point** is this. **They falsely claim that the basic human problem is racism, but they are WRONG! It is SIN**! **Romans 3:23-24** says,

"For all have sinned, and come short of the glory of God; 24 Being justified freely by his grace through the redemption that is in Christ Jesus:"

Romans 6:23 says,

"For the wages of sin is death; but the gift of God is eternal life through Jesus Christ our Lord."

I reject the Critical Race Theory because it is developed by man, it is based on worldly wisdom, it is based on deceit and it leaves Christ out. Paul warns us in **Colossians 2:8**,

"Beware lest any man spoil you through philosophy and vain deceit, after the tradition of men, after the rudiments of the world, and not after Christ."

LET'S EXAMINE A SECOND TEACHING OF CRT...

- Interest convergence or material determinism: White privilege – White people only give black people opportunities and freedoms when it is in their own interest.

"**White privilege**" refers to the myriad of social advantages, benefits, and courtesies that come with being a member of the dominant race.

The Interest-Convergence Thesis makes it literally <u>impossible for anyone with any racial privilege to do anything right because anything they do right must also have been motivated by self-interest</u>. When Critical Race Theory makes a demand of people with any form of racial privilege and they comply, they just make themselves more complicit in "racism" as Critical Race Theory sees it. By giving people no way out, Critical Race Theory becomes deeply manipulative and unable to be satisfied in its lists of demands. <u>Every effort is made to bully and intimidate white people to</u>

feel guilty for being white and apologize for it. Hence we have the origin of the phrase "**white guilt**."

Many white Hollywood actors/actresses have capitulated! Rosanne Arquette Tweeted,

> **"I am sorry I was born white and privileged. It disgusts me. And I feel so much shame."**

This is insane! In fact, I believe it is demonic (**James 3:15**). Neither you, nor I, nor anyone else had a choice as to the color we were born or where we were born. The Bible tells us that God *"hath made of one blood all nations of men for to dwell on all the face of the earth..."* (**Acts 17:26**). Regardless of our color we are all made in the image of God (**Gen. 1:27**) and God is no respecter of persons (**Acts 10:34, Rom. 2:11**). I refuse to have "white guilt" over how God made me. In fact, I praise the Lord for how He made me and this is the right thing to do according to the Bible - **Psalms 139:14** says,

> *"I will praise thee; for I am fearfully and wonderfully made: marvellous are thy works; and that my soul knoweth right well."*

It bears repeating: Regardless of our color, we are all made in the image of God (**Gen. 1:27**) and God is no respecter of persons (**Acts 10:34, Rom. 2:11**). Praise Him.

By the way, allow me to let you in on a secret. Only 13.4% of the population of the United States is black. According to CRT authors, Richard Delgado and Jean Stefancic, in their work *Critical Race Theory: An Introduction, 3rd edition*; pp.133-34,

> "the number of poor whites greatly exceeds that of poor minorities."

But they want to keep that quiet. CRT wants to keep the focus on the black minorities. <u>How hypocritical is that</u>? They WANT to keep the Blacks believing they are victimized! They do NOT want them believing what Martin Luther King, Jr. said – "I have a dream that...one day [we] will live in a nation where they will not be judged by the color of their skin, but by the **content of their character**" (August 28, 1963, Dr. Martin Luther King, Jr.).

We are told in God's Word that our thinking influences our behavior. **Prov. 23:7:**

> *"For as he thinketh in his heart, so is he...."*

That certainly is true. There are so many in the black community that believe "**the government owes us**!" They are like the men of Judah that said in **Jer. 18:12,**

> *"there is no hope: but we will walk after our own devices, and we will every one do the imagination of his evil heart."*

I was encouraged when I read what black author Carol Swain wrote. She is a retired professor of political science and law from Vanderbilt University. She wrote in her book *Race and Covenant,*

> "I was convinced that I was born into a land of opportunity. Despite being born black and poor, **I learned that one's attitude toward life was far more important than your race or**

social class in determining what you will accomplish."

If Swain had put her trust in Critical Race Theory, she might have given up early on. It might have persuaded her that the American system was stacked against any poor black woman, and that it was useless to try.

She went on to say that the Critical Race Theory will "only create anger, frustration and despondency" in the black youth it purports to help. She asks,

> "Should we keep telling them that they cannot thrive because of slavery in centuries past and white privilege today? Will this really help them? Is it even true? I don't think so. There are plenty of blacks, like me, who have come from dire circumstances and have risen above the circumstances of our birth."

CRT writers Richard Delgado and Jean Stefancic make clear what one of their key goals is – to

> "accept race conscious measures in employment and education, [and] **reparations should be**

paid by the government to Indians and blacks (*Critical Race Theory: An Introduction, 3rd edition*; p.158).

That is a completely unbiblical philosophy! God blesses work and diligence! We read in **Proverbs 10:4,**

> *"He becometh poor that dealeth with a slack hand: but the hand of the diligent maketh rich."* (See **Proverbs 12:24** & **13:4**).

The government does NOT owe anyone reparations! The Bible says in **2 Thessalonians 3:10,**

> *"For even when we were with you, this we commanded you, that if any would not work, neither should he eat."*

18

NOW, THE THIRD TEACHING OF CRT

- **Critical Race Theory is against free societies.**

CRT adherents see free societies and the ideals that make them work, (individualism, freedom, peace), as a kind of tacit [implied] conspiracy theory that we all participate in to keep racial minorities down. When its advocates accuse people of being "complicit in systems of racism," this is part of what they mean. The idea of individual autonomy, that people are free to make independent rational decisions; that is anathema to them. <u>Their goal is to do away with a free society</u> and **replace it** with <u>an arranged society as they see fit and force us all to go along with their ideas (socialism/communism)</u>. They hate individualism. Treating every person as an individual who is equal before God and equal before the law, and who is to be judged upon the content of their character and the merits of their work is considered a tactic to keep the racial minority down. CRT wants justice for the "group" at the expense of the individual!

Lynn Lemisko writes on page 193 of *Educator to Educator*, another education manual in Critical Social Justice programs:

"If democracy is about individual rights (justice for individuals), then social justice is about group rights (justice for groups). And for me there is a fundamental difference between the general notion of justice and the notion of social justice."

The plan of activists who advocate CRT is to make demands that people capitulate to their wishes. If they cannot get people to meet their demands, they will threaten trouble to get their way. If that does not work, they resort to violence as we have seen in Minneapolis, Chicago, Kenosha, Portland, Seattle, etc. But why? In their theory, there are only two groups of people, the privileged white oppressors and the black victimized oppressed. Gerald McDermott wrote:

"Even those who condemn racism are defined as oppressors if they belong to the wrong (white) group. People of color are victims of systemic oppression by whites and so are considered innocent in the cosmic war against good and evil. White people are "complicit" in white society's war against color, no matter what they say they believe or do." (Juicy Ecumenism: The

Institute on Religion and Democracy Blog; Gerald McDermott; February 11, 2020).

So, what is their remedy for ending racism? "It is through social revolution that unmakes the current society entirely and replaces it with something engineered by Critical Race Theory" adherents. (New Discourses; James Lindsay; June 12, 2020) If you think I am exaggerating allow me to give you an example. Seattle Council Woman Kashama Sawant says the Left is preparing the ground for a different kind of society. She went on to say,

> "Because we are coming for you and your rotten system. We are coming to dismantle this deeply oppressive, racist, sexist, violent utterly bankrupt system of capitalism. This police state. We cannot and will not stop until we overthrow it, and replace it with a world based, instead, on solidarity, genuine democracy, and equality: a socialist world."
> (https://www.realclearpolitics.com/video/202 0/07/07/seattle_city_councilwoman_we_will_ not_stop_until_we_overthrow_capitalism_rep lace_it_with_socialism.html)

ON TO THE FOURTH TEACHING OF CRT

- **Critical Race Theory believes our form of government, science, math, and reason are invalid because they are a part of white and Western culture.**

Christopher Rufo characterizes CRT in this way. "It teaches that the United States was founded on racism, slavery and oppression, and that our Constitutional structure, the words of the Declaration of Independence and even the law as it exists today are merely a cover story for racial oppression, dominance and hegemony [the dominance of one group over another]. The goal of CRT is to deconstruct the principles around the Western Canon of Law, around rationality and objectivity, around science and math and destroy all of those." (www.discovery.org/econ/2020/09/17/the-epoch-times-jan-jekielek-interviews-christopher-rufo-on-critical-race-theory)

President Trump got wind that CRT was being taught in various places in government. He issued an executive order banning federal contractors from conducting CRT training. He emphasized his desire to stop "efforts to indoctrinate government employees with divisive and harmful sex-and race-based ideologies." (Vox; *Critical race theory, and Trump's war on it, explained;* September 24, 2020 3.30 p.m.)

CRT ideologues reject science, reasoning, and math because they say they were predominantly produced by white Western men. They claim that knowledge is "socially constructed." By that they mean that knowledge reflects the values and interests of those who produced it. These ideologues falsely assert that white people's interests are primarily served by science (which is a racist statement in itself). That is just plain erroneous!

True science and math are objective, neutral and universal. Consider a key principle in math and science which is called **universality**. Universality in science and math says that it does not matter who solves a problem or who does the experiment, the result will always be the same.

So, what is the alternative since CRT teaches that black people aren't suited to or served by science or math? Delgado and Stefancic say that storytelling about their "lived experience" is the primary mode by which black people and Critical Race Theorists produce and advance knowledge. Do you see how bizarre this is? According to them, white

Western people learn and gain knowledge by science, math and reasoning (the power of the mind to think, understand and form judgments by a process of logic). <u>Storytelling of their lived experiences is more suited for racial minorities</u>. That statement is racist in itself!

While storytelling can be informative, to do away with reasoning, science and math only cripples the people CRT claims they want to help! As James Lindsay wrote,

> "It undermines their capacity for critical thinking, teaching them to see the world in an "us-versus-them" way that oppresses them, and associates them with harmful, negative stereotypes that rigorous methods are what the white people, and not black people, use."

CONCLUSION

The **Critical Race Theory** is a doctrine of the Devil! Our Lord said, *"Blessed are the peacemakers* (**Mat. 5:9**). The advocates of CRT are NOT peacemakers but troublemakers. Our nation was founded upon Old Testament & New Testament principles. But as people turned away from the Bible, worldly, sensual, and demonic philosophies have taken its place. Paul warned about this time coming. He said in **2 Timothy 3:13**,

> *"evil men and seducers shall wax worse and worse, deceiving, and being deceived."*

He continued in **2 Timothy 4:3-4**,

> *"For the time will come when they will not endure sound doctrine; but after their own lusts shall they heap to themselves teachers, having itching ears; And they shall turn away their ears from the truth, and shall be turned unto fables."*

We are living in the days that Paul warned Timothy about. The advocates and adherents to CRT are teaching fables to advance their own lustful agenda and they will be judged by God. Psalms 11:5-6 says, *"The LORD trieth the righteous: but the wicked and him that loveth violence his soul hateth. Upon the wicked he shall rain snares, fire and brimstone, and an horrible tempest: this shall be the portion of their cup."*

Don't be deceived into accepting the demonic doctrine of Critical Race Theory.

Resources

Critical Race Theory: An Introduction, 3rd edition

Juicy Ecumenism: The Institute on Religion and Democracy Blog; Gerald McDermott; February 11, 2020

New Discourses; James Lindsay; June 12, 2020

Is Critical Race Theory Compatible with Christian Faith? By Gerald McDermott; February 11, 2020

Race and Covenant, Acton Books, 2020

Critical Race Theory – What Is It - (www.patheos.com/blogs/northamptonseminar/2020/02/05/critical -race-theory-i-what-is-it)

Wokeism at Work: How "Critical Theory" and Anti-Racism Training Divide America; July 27, 2020 -- (www.youtube.com/watch?v=D6mwDvEqpl0&feature=emb_r el_pause)

www.discovery.org/econ/2020/09/17/the-epoch-times-jan-jekielek-interviews-christopher-rufo-on-critical-race-theory/

"Well," **you** **ask,** **"how** **would** **I** **know?"** Thank God, according to the Bible, not only can you *know*, but you can *choose* where you will spend eternity.

Now we all believe – or at least most claim to believe – in the Bible as God's Word. We believe in eternity and know that life is short. The Bible itself asks, "What is your life? It is even a vapor, that appeareth for a little time, and then vanisheth away" (James 4:14).

Many claim to believe in heaven and in hell, yet, unfortunately, show little concern over their eternal destiny. We are far more concerned about this life than the next, yet we know that eternity is endless. The Word of God describes it as being "forever and ever" (Revelation 22:5).

Just think . . . an eternity to be spent forever, either in the perfect paradise called heaven or in the terrible torments of hell.

Surely we'll agree that it is just good sense to prepare for eternity now, before it is forever too late. God says, "It is appointed unto men once to die, but after this the judgment" (Hebrews 9:27).

"Well," you say, "I believe in God, go to church, and live the best I can. What else can I do?"

Now believing in God, attending church, and doing one's best are all admirable; yet, according to the Word of God, the Holy Bible, these *cannot* get us to heaven. Neither, according to God, can our church membership, baptism, confirmation, nor our good deeds attain for us eternal life.

But God has provided an answer to the matter of life and death, heaven and hell. It is an answer so simple it is frequently overlooked.

A religious leader named Nicodemus came to Jesus one night for help. Jesus told him, "You must be born again," and expanded this to include all of us by stating quite emphatically, "Except a man be born again, he cannot see the kingdom of God" (John 3:3). Pretty dogmatic perhaps, but these are the words of Christ Himself.

Some today, like Nicodemus, will ask, "How can a man be born when he is old? Can he enter the second time into his mother's womb, and be born?" (John 3:4). But Jesus answers, "That which is born of the flesh is flesh; and that which is born of Spirit is spirit" (John 3:6), stating again that one must experience a spiritual rebirth in order to enter heaven – "You *must* be born again" (John 3:7).

Now, have *you* been born again? Have you experienced this spiritual rebirth? This is the one thing, according to the Bible, that will determine your eternal destiny.

So, for those who really want to know how to be born again, here is the answer from God's Word.

We must **recognize that we are sinners,** that we've all violated God's law. The Bible says, "All have sinned, and come short of the glory of God . . . There is not a just man upon earth, that doeth good, and sinneth not . . . If we say that we have no sin, we deceive ourselves, and the truth is not in us" (Romans 3:23, 10; Ecclesiastes 7:20; I John 1:8, 10).

We must **repent of our sins.** The Bible says that God "commandeth all men everywhere to repent" (Acts 17:30). Jesus said, "Except you repent, you shall all likewise perish" (Luke 13:3). And it is not so difficult to repent as we pause to think of what our sins have cost God. It was for our sins that God, the Creator and King of this universe, left His

30

home in heaven and came to earth in the Person of the Lord Jesus to suffer and bleed and die – that we might be forgiven. "Hereby perceive we the love of God, because He laid down His life for us" (I John 3:16). Then Jesus rose from the dead, proving His victory over sin and death.

We must *receive* **Christ into our hearts and lives as our Savior.** We read in the first chapter of John, speaking of the Lord Jesus, "He was in the world, and the world was made by Him, and the world knew Him not. He came unto His own, and His own received Him not. But as many as *received* Him, to them gave He power to become the sons of God, even to them that believe on His name" (John 1:10-12). The moment we open our hearts to the Lord Jesus and place our complete trust in Him – and Him alone – as our Savior, God promises to forgive our sins, save our soul, and reserve for us a home in heaven. Then, on the authority of the Word of God, **we can *know* where we'll spend eternity.** God says, "These things have I written unto you that believe on the name of the Son of God; that you may *know* that you *have* eternal life" (I John 5:13). And Jesus promises, "He that heareth My word, and believeth on Him that sent Me, hath everlasting life, and shall not come into condemnation; but is passed from death unto life" (John 5:24).

Now, are you willing to settle the matter of your eternal destiny? Will you do it? You can, right this moment. I sincerely hope that you will.

(*Used by permission of The American Tract Society, Garland, Texas*

Available From –

+ **✝** +
Dr. David L. Brown
P.O. Box 173
Oak Creek, Wisconsin 53154
PastorDavidLBrown@gmail.com

ABOUT THE AUTHOR

David L. Brown was born in Michigan. He came to know Christ as his Savior as the result of a Sunday school teacher throwing away the liberal curriculum, teaching through the book of Romans, and sharing the Gospel. He has been married to Linda for 49 years. She was a young lady from his home church.

David attended a Michigan University then transferred to a Christian University and Seminary where he completed a Bachelor's Degree in Social Science and Theology. He holds a Master's Degree in Theology, and Ph.D. in History, specializing in the history of the English Bible.

Since December 1979, he has been the Pastor of the First Baptist Church of Oak Creek, Wisconsin (an independent, fundamental, Baptist Church using the King James Bible and conservative music). Previous to that, he pastored an independent Baptist Church in Michigan for five years, was an assistant pastor for 4 years, and served with his wife as short-term missionaries in Haiti.

Dr. Brown is the president of the *King James Bible Research Council*:
(www.kjbresearchcouncil.com),
an organization dedicated to promoting the King James Bible and its underlying texts and other traditional text translations around the world in a solid and sensible way.

He is also the president of *Logos Communication Consortium, Inc*.
(www.logosresourcepages.org),
a research organization that produces a large variety of materials warning Christians of present dangers in our culture. He is also the vice president of the *Midwest Independent Baptist Pastor's Fellowship*, a fellowship of independent Baptist pastors, missionaries, and evangelists from fourteen upper Midwest states.

Dr. Brown is the Curator of the *Christian Heritage Bible Collection* and regularly takes his rare Bible, manuscript and artifact collection to fundamental Baptist Churches teaching and preaching on the history of our English Bible, showing how God has preserved His Word(s), and why we should use the King James Bible.

He also serves as a consultant for individuals, museums, colleges, universities, and seminaries that desire to acquire or have collections of biblical manuscripts and Bibles. He is an antiquarian book dealer with contacts around the world.

SOME OF HIS OTHER PUBLICATIONS INCLUDE:

1. *The Indestructible Book,* a 500 page, hardback with a cover
2. *The Indestructible Book,* a 500 page, perfect bound book
3. *God's Blueprint For Marriage & Family*, a perfect bound book, 108 pages
4. *The Defined Geneva Bible, New Testament, With Modern Spelling*, Editor, hardback, 344 pages
5. *The Geneva Bible, Old Testament, With Modern Spelling,* Editor, hardback, 970 pages.
6. *The Dark Side of Halloween*
7. *The 1576 Tyndale New Testament and Biography*, Hardback, 540 pages, Editor
8. Editor - *The Bible Source Book*
9. *Gaslighted, You Are Being Gaslighted,* a Booklet, 32 pages, concerning the lies and propaganda perpetrated on America.

He can be contacted at:

Dr. David L. Brown
8044 S. Verdev Dr.
Oak Creek, WI. 53154
Phone: 414-768-9754
Email: PastorDavidLBrown@gmail.com